11 Simple Rules
for Real Property Profits

11 Simple Rules
for Real Property Profits

"Deals that win, deals that lose."

ROLAND HAERTL

ISBN 978-0-578-67843-6

Library of Congress Control Number: 2020907887

Book cover and interior design by Ray Rhamey

Contents

Part 1

Basics: Prerequisites

Part 2

11 Simple Rules

Acknowledgments

This book is the product of a few years of thinking about it and then finally reviewing several previously considered concepts, resulting in this "HOW TO" book squeezed into the time frame of a forced sequestration due to the Covid-19 virus which offered almost uninterrupted production time.

I want to thank my long-term friend and partner who generated the initial idea twelve years ago, John Thelen.

For suggestions and proofreading. I want to thank my wife, Leslie Kolisch, and Brian Ekiss, Mary Ekiss, Scott Wykoff, Scott Howard, my children Jennifer, Helen, and Jeffrey for their encouragement.

I especially thank my grandson Gavin Doyle for his continuing advice and encouragement based on his own publishing and marketing experience.

Lastly, my thanks go to Ray Rhamey, my editor, for guiding a novice and making the product presentable.

May 2020

Roland Haertl

Introduction

This book is not intended to replace the detailed study of and familiarization with the plethora of excellent real estate literature available. It should be read as a synopsis of rules garnered in deal-making.

This book does not address or consider long-term real estate investment in income properties, not because these are not profitable, but because they are unexciting after implementation. Their management tasks are exactly that, "management tasks."

The book focuses on a few key factors affecting failure or success in real estate projects. These are documented by actual experience and projects that support and explain the stated "rules." Some of the "vignettes" fit the stipulated rules and advice better than others.

This is not a guidebook to learn all there is to know about the real estate industry, i.e. methodology of property valuation, long-term investment planning, financing approaches and systems, or "complete investment techniques." That information is abundantly available in hundreds of books. The reader of this booklet should already be familiar with the literature and advice contained there.

Your interest in this booklet is different.

You are interested in real estate and are wondering how you might participate in the "successes" in real estate you hear about everywhere and frequently. You are not risk-averse but want to familiarize yourself with the varying levels of risk in alternative real estate ventures. You have financial resources and want to know how you can leverage them into profits.

This will require your action. It will include investment of money, time and risk. You will need to involve yourself in "deals" requiring varying levels of money, time and risk that have no guarantee of success. When and if successful, however, the satisfaction of accomplishment and measurement in financial reward can be euphoric.

Basic rules and axioms are presented and discussed as advice. More detailed recommendations are discussed in the main body of the book and are backed up by project histories. This book is written to summarize a lifetime in the real estate "deals" sector, and, drawing on it, crystallize the conclusions in a few basic rules.

More than forty years in the real estate development by Roland Haertl, an engineer, broker and developer, support his conclusions. He lives and works in the Pacific Northwest of the United States.

Origin of this Book

During my more than fifty years in business, I was predominantly active in the engineering and construction industry through various businesses. My real estate activity was mostly reactive to approaches by brokers who would contact me with "deals."

Brokers contacted me first because they knew that I never tried to renegotiate their commission. Effort should be fairly rewarded. If a proposed transaction is feasible, it works with a 4.5 % fee and a 5.5% fee.

One of the brokers approaching me with prospective transactions was John Thelen, a long-time acquaintance, fellow handball player and real estate broker. From 1995 forward, he approached me with several projects. I acquired some of them and one with John Thelen as a partner.

In 2005 and 2006, I received attractive offers to sell my projects and a separate offer on the partner project with John Thelen. By May 2006 we had liquidated all projects, excluding our homes. In November 2007 we congratulated ourselves over a lunch and made an agreement which we called "Deals Anonymous."

John had always lived by "the deal." I less so. Both of us liked the thrill of a potential deal. I had analyzed 32 potential projects before I invested in my first one in 1970. John had been involved in a comparable number of land deals.

In mid-2007, when the real estate market showed accelerating signs of weakness, John and I decided, and vowed to each other, to not do any more "deals." "Deals Anonymous" was born.

The rules are: "If one of use gets the urge to do a deal, he is to call the other, explain his urge, and be talked out of it. If the 'deal proposer' talks about a deal for longer than 10 minutes, he owes the other $2,500. If he proceeds with the deal, he owes $25,000."

We mentioned this agreement to several of our friends, acquaintances, and legal and financial consultants. It was always met with laughter and a request for membership in the informal "club." In 2009, when speaking on the phone with my accountant, he said: "I had three of my clients say, 'I should have talked to those Deals Anonymous guys and had them talk me out of one of my deals'."

The arrival of the Covid-19 corona virus in the US at the end of 2019 has set off a more severe and faster downturn of the US economy than the one of 2007-2009. At the time of this writing, April 2020, the severity of the downturn and its duration are not predictable. They could far exceed the 2007-2009 time span and the severity of that recession. This pandemic and its effects differ from the last financial calamity by the addition of high unemployment and an overwhelming increase in poverty.

Opportunities for deals and profits in real estate will become available. Dealmakers and investors, however, are facing the added dilemma of avoiding social amorality by taking advantage of the newly impoverished. Careful planning and deal structuring as in 2009-2010 can benefit the new wave of the needy while presenting profit opportunities for investors if performed in a socially responsible way.

On a barstool in 2010, I had a casual conversation with the neighbor on the next seat. He asked about my profession and I asked him about his. He said, "Real estate investor." I inquired about his present project.

"We identified an investment opportunity in the city of Detroit, Michigan. We have connected with a big financial entity that will fund the purchase of whole street tracts of foreclosed and abandoned houses we can buy at deep discounts. We will then market them to new renters. Their main responsibility is to keep them maintained after the repairs we performed. Their incentives are several: very reasonable low rent, an option to purchase the house at a preset fixed price after a 5-to-7-year option period and, third, a portion of their rent would be paid into an equity reserve fund that, upon exercise of their purchase option, would apply to the necessary down payment."

I was duly impressed with the balancing of financial benefits between the venture investors and the renters/potential purchasers.

It is this type of structure and thinking that will be needed for an exit out of the present looming crisis. The risks during this period are big. The potential profits in new deals are huge.

If you want to be active in real estate, the involvement in "deals" is unavoidable.

Their success and failure depend on many factors and how they and inevitable problems are addressed and solved. In this book I discuss actions enhancing success and others increasing the risk of non-success and/or failure. During my activity in the real estate market, I made decisions which put me into bankruptcy in 1991. Recovering from it consumed a few years of hard work and revision of my approach to real estate investment. The "rules" in this book are based on real project decisions and their results.

Consider them and apply them at your own risk. Enjoy!

Prerequisites

1. Are you a "Real Estate Deal" personality?
2. Is your "Team" ready?
3. Are your "Partners and Partner Relationships" robust?

11 Simple Rules

1. Do not rely on deals for your living expenses.
2. Do not "need a deal."
3. Use as much OPM as possible.
4. Beware of Small Markets.
5. Be prepared to walk away from a deal.
6. Buy property for less than you think you can sell it.
7. Define your deal horizon/timing early in the venture.
8. Plan your alternative exit strategies.
9. Be prepared to sell: any profit is a profit.
10. Keep it simple.
11. Keep control of the deal.

$ $ $

Time waits for no one.

(tempus neminem manet)

Lucius Annaeus Seneca ("The Younger")

4 B.C. - 65 A.D.

Part 1
Basics: Prerequisites

Prerequisite 1

Are you a "real estate deal" personality?

Risk Tolerance

Real estate ventures are founded on land and improved by "brick and mortar" structures. Their nature is "inert." The industry has a high inertia and resists quick change of direction through management philosophy.

This inertia inserts extra risk into every real estate transaction. Time and timing of decisions is a significant factor in success or failure of a venture. Careful and thorough analysis of a venture will mitigate risks and quantify them. Risks cannot be avoided.

Ask yourself: "Can I live with the risk inherent in transactions? Can I deal with the stress connected with the monetary risks?"

Decision Maker

While real estate ventures typically do not require daily decisions, the decisions required are more than finetuning of operations. They can be "all or nothing" decisions.

Ask yourself: "Can I make these clearly, decisively, and live with them?"

Entrepreneur

Real estate ventures are entrepreneurial. They require leadership, wide-range input from others, inventiveness, and initiative.

Ask yourself: "Am I willing and able to lead?"

During the recession of 2008/09 a banker, an accountant, and a developer were forced to move under a bridge.

The banker found a cardboard box, unfolded it and moved in. The accountant did the same next to the banker's box. The developer found himself a box, unfolded it, placed it on top of the other two boxes, put up a big sign: "New penthouse available for Sale."

Stress Tolerance

Lastly, the stress of the swing from optimism to pessimism in the time progression of a real estate venture can impact your sleep, health, mental balance, and relationships with the persons close to you, especially spouses and life partners.

Ask yourself: "Am I able to compartmentalize these stresses and live with them?" "Is my life partner?"

The ideal partner of a developer: "Honey, I can't seem to be able to go to sleep. Why don't you tell me about your day at work?"

A California Highway Patrol stops a driver on I5. "Please show me your Real Estate License."

"You mean Driver's License, right?"

"No, not everyone in California has a Driver's License, but everybody has a Real Estate License."

Prerequisite 2

Is your team ready?

Support Team

Attorney, Accountant, Broker, Banker, Engineer/Planner, Contractor(s), Title Insurance Company. And your friends at the regulatory agencies.

The assembly or at least consideration of assembly of a team which contains legal advisor, accountant, tax advisor, broker, engineer/planner, contractor is typical.

One essential team member is not always included: Title Insurance Company and title officer. They should always be the early contact to obtain base data on a project.

Project

I paid dearly for that omission on my part at least once. The setting: in 1970 my engineering firm was to design and obtain building permits for a Mini Storage project in Tacoma, Washington. At that time in the infancy of the ministorage industry, buildings were one-story storage units at ground level and accessible from adjacent drives. Buildings were from 20 to 50 feet wide and 100 to 200 feet long. Our developer client furnished a print of a preliminary property survey. We based our development and permit plans on it.

The survey print also showed an outline of a 40' x 250' rectangle in the middle of the survey map, almost splitting the property in half, but not otherwise described. Our permit plans included a storage building E taking up that rectangle. When I submitted the permit application the plans examiner of the city approved the project but stated that he could not issue a building permit for E without stating a reason. I pressed for a permit for E which he reluctantly granted and issued.

The project went into construction. While on a vacation in Mexico City I received a call from my Tacoma project owner: "Roland, remember building E? It sits on an easement." Everything fell into place from past events.

The holder of the easement consented to relocate it for additional compensation.

I could have avoided this potentially expensive mistake by obtaining a preliminary title report early in the project.

Include the title insurance company early in any project as a team member.

$ $ $

A balloonist is blown off-course. He decides to land in a field, next to a road. He does not know where he is. He hails a car coming down the road. The driver stops and gets out.

Balloonist:" Can you tell me where I am?"

"Yes, of course," says the driver. "You just landed your balloon and, with this wind, you have obviously been blown off course. You are in the top field on John Dawson's farm, 10 miles from Charlotte. John will be plowing the field next week and sow wheat. There is a bull in the field. It is behind you and about to attack you."

At that moment the bull reaches the balloonist and tosses him over the next fence. The balloonist is not hurt, gets up, dusts himself off and says to the motorist: "I can tell you are an appraiser."

"Amazing," says the motorist, "you are right. How did you know that?"

"I employ appraisers," says the balloonist. "The information you gave me was detailed, precise, and accurate. Most of it was useless, and it arrived far too late to be of any help." (adapted from Chris O'Connor, C. Rutenberg Realty, Inc.)

Prerequisite 3

Are your Partners and Partner Relationships robust?

Ideally, you would prefer to conceive and complete your real estate investment project without complicating the project structure and decision process by the inclusion of partners.

Partners add complexity to the decision process. They also improve the quality of the resulting decisions and the general risk of the project. You should first define if you need a partner, want a partner, and what type he or she should be. Financial? Expertise? Participating property owners? Keep the number of partners as small as possible. Even "small" partners can easily become a problem for several reasons. One of my clients is still carrying partners with ownership percentages of less than 1% in some of his projects.

There is a solution to this potential issue: Solomon's Rule.

Here is how it works:

In the partner buyout provision of the partnership, it should state that any partner has the right to make an offer of buyout to any other partner. The offer must be a monetary offer. The partner receiving the offer in turn now has the right to buy out the offeror on the same terms and price.

This arrangement keeps the partners honest. It can also be used to dissolve a problematic partnership by making a low buyout offer which might induce the offeree to reverse the transaction. I have used this contract clause several times, avoiding acrimony over buyout negotiations.

Project

In 2003 a married couple, an engineer and an accountant known to me for 30 years, had become residential builders but had no experience in land development.

They approached me to partner with them, 50/50, in the land development, for them to purchase the developed lots for residential buildout by them. 50% of the houses were built, most sold on schedule. The husband died after a short illness.

Over the next year the widow became increasingly erratic in her decision-making, creating problems for the partnership relations. I made the decision to dissolve the partnership.

I offered the widow for purchase the remaining developed lots at about 70% of her perceived and the bank's appraised value. She reversed the offer and bought me out within two weeks in 2007.

Conclusion

Solomon's Rule should be a clause in every partnership and should be part of any joint venture or corporate entity.

A client asked me for advice: "You know we have about 60 employees who, in the receiving building, select the potatoes coming off the truck for the French fry product by removing low-quality potatoes. They stand along the moving belts. One complains of being too hot, the next one is too cold. How do we solve this?"

I thought, then: "We have an acoustic ceiling in the building. Let's install a thermostat controller behind each sorter on the wall, run a conduit from it into the ceiling and just terminate it there."

"You are crazy. Let's try it."

We installed the fake controllers. A few weeks later the client called me: "They are all happy. Each employee has total control."

Conclusion

Belief is reality. Placebos work.

Some of my OPM sources have retained me from time to time to examine problems at properties in their portfolio. One called: "Two-story frame apartments, T1-11 plywood siding, belly band at the top of the first story. Please review the siding, T1-11, above the belly band. It is buckling out at the bottom of the upper T1-11 panel, just above the belly band. Architect tells me we need to reside the project, $100,000 to 150.000."

At my inspection, I noticed that the buckling occurred only on the south and west side of the buildings. That made me suspect that the cause might be the exposure to the sun, resulting in expansion of the 9-foot plywood siding. The siding panels were flashed at the belly band with a metal "Z" flashing over the belly band. The siding crew was lazy and rested the panels on the "Z" flashing's horizontal, slightly out-sloping leg, then nailed them to the framing. No gap between the flashing and the bottom of the panels.

When I calculated the thermal expansion of the panels in direct sunlight, it was large enough to cause the plywood panels to elongate in the only way they could, vertically at the flashing. The sloping flashing pushed the bottom edge downslope, buckling the panels.

Solution: shorten the panels at the bottom to provide for panel expansion. Total cost $30,000. Total Savings based on architect's estimate: $70,000 to $120,000.

Conclusion

Team relationships are essential and should be maintained for the long-term benefit of everybody.

Part 2:
11 Simple Rules

Rule 1

Do not rely on deals for your living expenses

Real estate investment projects are planned to move along a projected schedule. Expected returns are based on that schedule. The planned schedule rarely matches reality.

Even the most-detailed task schedule stretches in real time. The delay in completion delays income cashflow, increases costs, and lowers the real rate of return.

This unreliability of timing of cash flow clearly speaks against reliance on it for living expenses. Here are two examples of time delays, albeit extreme.

Project 1:

In 1970, a client asked me to perform a preliminary site constraint to decide on the purchase of a 1,064-acre package of several contiguous raw land parcels located in the City of Portland and two county jurisdictions. Preliminary interviews and inquiries with 28 regulatory and service agencies revealed many issues, but no insurmountable obstacles. Existing zoning was for single-family residential development of 20,000-square-foot lots.

We, four partners, formed a partnership, obtained OPM ("Other People's Money") and purchased the property. Preliminary planning proceeded. Regulatory, jurisdictional and political issues arose immediately (traffic, utility services, codes, environmental concerns and, naturally, NIMBYs, i.e. "Not In My Back Yard").

We also concluded that the "half-acre" zoning was socially and politically (school population) irresponsible and the project should serve a more "urban/suburban" population.

Studies and analyses by our planning team confirmed all our representations and secured necessary services. Upon the filing of our petition for a zoning change to the higher density in 1971, people "far and nigh" rose in revolt. Hearings had to be relocated to higher capacity venues. The NIMBYs filed a lawsuit. 14 years later, in 1985, the Oregon

Court of Appeals gave us a clean bill of approval.

The project was sold in 1985 and completed 30 years later with 2,000 residential units, school, etc.

By 1985 the huge legal fees of between $500,00 and $1,000,000 had forced resignation of 2 of the 4 original partners. I also sold my interest in 1984, making some money.

Project 2:

One of my clients purchased a large parcel in Southwest Washington in 1980. A residential community around a golf course was developed. The original development plan contained one parcel designated for future townhouse development. My client decided in 1995 to propose to develop that parcel into single-family residential units rather than townhouses.

The neighborhood associations decided to oppose development of the site. My client abandoned the plan. In 2012 he decided to refile for development into 12 single-family lots after the property was annexed to the

City of Battle Ground. One NIMBY filed a lawsuit. During the next three years it went all the way to the Washington State Court of Appeals in three steps. At all levels the NIMBYs lost.

My client developed the parcel into 12 lots which sold in December 2019.

Conclusion

Do not rely on a proposed schedule and projected pay-out for a living. It took 39 years to turn the land into cash.

In 1986, the Development Commission of the City of Portland called me and requested that I talk to an inexperienced property owner whose project the commission would like to proceed and who needed some guidance.

The commission could not get involved because of potential political conflicts. The property owners retained me to manage the process.

The soils/foundation consultant concluded that the addition of 3 stories to the old tire storage building would, due to its underlying soil, require a piling system with piles penetrating 60 feet into the subsoil, making the project unfeasible. I questioned that conclusion. My calculations showed that the loaded tire storage had imposed a load 30% higher than the 3-story addition would without any adverse effects of settlement.

How to prove it?

I had the contractors build a "bathtub" on the second floor and filled it with four feet of water, adding a weight equivalent to three stories. After six weeks of monitoring and measuring any movement, one column showed a settlement of .125 inches. Proof successful. Project successful.

Conclusion

This is a prime example of teamwork and partnership relation and inventiveness.

Rule 2

Do not "need a deal!"

When considering a new project, ask yourself why you want to do it.

Is it a project that shows all signs of "positives"? Or are some of the factors identified in the "hope" category?

Are you sufficiently critical in your evaluation of the feasibility?

Do you need a deal?

If the answer to this last question is "yes", run away from the deal as fast as you can. Keep in mind that "need" blurs rational thinking.

Analysis is tinged by hope. Projections of cashflow are on the sunny side. Expenses are underestimated. Markets are overly optimistically assessed.

It is the path to failure.

The following story is a prime example.

Project

In 1982 I had just sold my company. My income was far into the future. My cash flow was insufficient to cover my living expenses. I came across a potential historic rehab building that looked promising.

During detailed analysis, some problems appeared. I ignored them with the hope that they were insignificant.

My partner and I secured acquisition funds and a bank loan for improvements. The bank appraisal was $3,900,000 completed. The loan of $2,500.000 resulted in a Loan to Value ratio of .64.

Lease-up was slow. My partner brought in a proposal from a prospective brew pub, with a requirement of a $1,500,000 estimated buildout cost. After discussion we turned down that deal. Brewpubs were still untested. In hindsight this would have been a hit. The building would have fit perfectly in its layout and historic imagery. A killer mistake.

The rental receipts of the building never achieved the projected level neither in the office or retail areas.

I finally had to acknowledge that the uncertainty and qualms I had suppressed during the acquisition phase were becoming reality.

In 1989 the bank notified us that it re-evaluated its loan portfolio, including our project. The result of the re-appraisal was a new value of $1,900,000. The bank required that we reduce the loan to that amount.

This, combined with some other not directly connected cashflow issues, forced my personal bankruptcy in 1990. I could no longer make any deals for seven years, till 1997.

Conclusion

Do not put yourself in "need a deal" and then implement one.

Historic (or older buildings) pose problems with lay-out when re-purposed to new uses and occupancy needs. When we installed the tenant improvements in this historic building the space layout resulted in a dead-end corridor. I measured it at 21 feet in length. It exceeded allowable code length of 18 feet.

I had always had good relations with the Building department and its inspectors. I called for help to the project inspector. He visited the space affected, laid down his tape to measure the corridor length: "16 feet. You do not have a problem."

Conclusion

Personal relationships and professional courtesies are appreciated and valued by all parties.

Rule 3

Use as much OPM as possible

Other People's Money. It serves several purposes:

It fills gaps in your cash requirement.

It reduces your risk.

It allows you to lower the L/V (Loan to Value) ratio in financing, making financing easier.

It may be the only way to get started.

The key to being successful to raise OPM is to establish a reputation/track record of commitment and performance to the OPM source. The credibility thus established serves to make long-term venture-inclined money sources available.

It is essential to communicate regularly and straightforwardly with your OPM sources about the status, progress and financial condition of the project.

There is no substitute for a successful project completion.

The agreements between a developer and the OPM source may be structured around different methods of compensation for the OPM provider. The OPM source may receive a front fee (in the form of cash payment or a discounted amount of the capital).

It may become a creditor (lender) at a defined interest rate on its capital payable at a certain date or defined event.

It may become a participating venture party at a predetermined percentage in the wind-up phase of the deal (however the wind-up phase may be defined).

As a receiver of OPM one should beware of interest charges on the capital furnished, either payable periodically or accruing till the wind-up phase of the deal.

At a stated annual interest rate of 5%, compounding annually, a $1,000,000 capital contribution will grow to $1,280,000 after 5 years, a short time frame for any project, to $1,630,000 over 10 years if the schedule stretches that much.

Project 1

1971 Office Building, frame construction, 12,000 SF, 2-story. Located on SW Pennoyer St. in Portland. My architect partner and I had just sold a commercial lot and were looking at acquiring and developing this property for an office building. We were short of some equity and I approached two old acquaintances/friends with farm ownership in Eastern Oregon for additional funding.

They agreed. I went to local bank with a slightly playful venture name:

Pennoyer Land and Cattle Company, with the connection to farming and old Portland history (Pennoyer). The banker placed the loan to a Canadian bank which, he said, liked the entity name. It also offered the potential of a 20% stock up of the loan in case unforeseen problems arose.

We developed, constructed, leased the building space and sold, due to request of cashing out by the OPM equity partners, the building in 1978. Satisfaction all around.

Project 2

In 1978 a banker friend called and offered me the land parcel approved for an industrial park in Southwest Portland in which he was a controlling partner. In early 1979 I raised the necessary OPM from an outside source to acquire the property. The seller carried back a small contract.

In August 1979 I developed some anxiety about the economy and decided to offer the project for sale. I sold it under a land contract with substantial monthly payments to a construction contractor in Beaverton who was looking for a buildout project. The sales contract stipulated monthly payments due on the first of each month commencing October 1, 1979. The first payment was made October 1, the second November 6 the third December 9. When the January 1, 1980 payment, due January 1, had not been paid by January 9, 1980 I made a phone call to the buyer. He answered the phone, I identified myself and I asked about the overdue payment. He "I don't know when I will pay you, maybe never." I asked my secretary to listen in and asked him to repeat that statement, which he did. I hung up and called my lawyer, instructing him to file a default and foreclosure notice in Washington County the same day. He did. It was served the next day. On the following day I received a check in the full amount of the sales contract, paying off 100%. I paid off my OPM funder and the balance of the bank.

In the following two years, interest rates rose drastically. The industrial park project did not get completed till 1995. An unsubstantiated hunch turned into this successful transaction.

Conclusion

OPM has great advantages and its sources should be cultivated. Care needs to be taken with the compensation terms to the money source.

Rule 4

Beware of Small Markets

"Small market" usually refers to small numbers of people in an area or jurisdiction. "Small markets" may also mean that certain real estate products will receive limited acceptance by buyers in that area even when a large population base exists. We have seen that for condominium and loft products.

It is important to quantify the market for niche products through focus groups and market research.

Here are examples for each "small market."

Project 1

In 1978 I was offered a small undeveloped property in one of Portland's prime residential/apartment areas. The property was zoned for 24 rental/apartment units. I believed that the location would be ready for single family townhouses and would achieve top sale prices. This was to be the first project of its type in the inner city.

We designed, constructed and marketed the four houses. We sold all four within six weeks at full price to "name" buyers. While the project was an outright and immediate success, I was uncertain of the market depth at that time for that product. 7 years later the inner-city condominium wave commenced.

Project 2

From 1976 forward my company had been constructing several industrial projects in Umatilla County. In 1983 a broker in Hermiston, Oregon inquired about my interest in developing a 40 residential-unit subdivision in Hermiston. The concept was to build out a subdivision and sale of finished lots to local builders. We decided to split the project into two phases, each of 20 lots, and finish the first phase. We obtained a development loan, installed the improvements for 20 lots. All 20 lots were sold within one year. We then decided to complete the second phase by installing all improvements.

We sold the second phase lots over the next 10 long years.

Conclusion

We had absorbed hundred percent of the existing single-family lot market with the first phase of 20 lots. Beware of small markets.

The townhouse project above was sitting on basalt bedrock. Site excavation produced some boulders up to 4 feet in size. Their removal depended on equipment availability. One night one rolled off the site for about 20 feet to the street below and flattened the VW beetle parked there. The car was the only fatality. It brought a few smiles to our faces seeing the boulder faceted like a gemstone by the crushed roof of the beetle.

Rule 5

Be prepared to walk away from a deal

It is difficult to abandon a project on which you have spent much time and energy, not even considering the money. The reasons for walking away vary.

You may discover a defect in the data that makes you question other assumptions. Or the parameters to obtain control change several times during negotiations to make you question the prospect of successfully resolving future problems and disagreements.

Project 1

In 1986 I became interested in the changes looming in the mobile home park industry. The rental/cash flow/landholding philosophy was changing due to underlying land values increasing for potential "higher" end uses.

I identified a 120-unit mobile home park in a medium size Oregon town. It was for sale at a price that met my parameters. I obtained operating data from the owner and regulatory agency information from several data sources. The operating data furnished by the owner looked reasonable except for one flag: water consumption charges. They appeared quite low. Water service was provided by a large regional utility company. I questioned the seller.

He at first appeared a little uncomfortable with the question. After pressing him further he explained that he had two taps into the water supply line. He paid for one for approximately 30 units. The other 90 units were served by an illegal and fraudulent tap into the main supply line without an approved and recognized meter. He was cheating the utility company and had done so for years.

I thanked the owner for the information and abandoned the project immediately.

Project 2

In 1989 I became interested in the potential of redevelopment of a small restaurant-occupied, centrally located site. After I approached the widow of the long-term owner, she and I executed a short-term purchase option agreement. The option required an option payment of $170,000, within 90 days. The option payment would then allow me to exercise the purchase within 90 days after the option payment with the balance of $1,530,000.

I was trying to do this project with 100% OPM. I therefore needed to identify a venture partner who had the willingness and capacity to finance approximately $5,000,000. This would require an aggressive pursuit of an investment partner.

During the pre-option time, I wasted several weeks by not concentrating on the timeframe to raise the OPM. I would soon have to decide whether to come up with the option payment myself or abandon the project.

When the option payment became due, I put hope before reality and paid for it myself. I was not able to obtain OPM within the option period and eventually had to abandon the project and lose the option payment.

With more critical thinking I should have abandoned this project before the option payment was due.

Conclusion

When in doubt, walk away from a deal.

In 1969 I was made aware that an apartment developer was contemplating purchasing an existing golf course on the Oregon coast and develop housing around it. I was familiar with the golf course and its annual flooding from seasonal storms, which put major portions under water. I called him. After documenting additional data for him, he walked away from the project.

Rule 6

Buy property for less than you think you can sell it

You will not consider a real estate project unless you believe that you can make a profit. Real estate investment has the prospect of significant profits more than any other industry. Its focus on specific locations simplifies entry and enables single entrepreneurs to participate. This book does not address the long-term investment in projects that produce their profits in cash flow from rents or other use fees. This book only addresses the realization of a gain or profit through its sale.

In 1970 one of my clients, in a conversation over projects and her landholdings, located in North and

Central America, remarked: "I own a lot of green. It is just the wrong kind of green. We need to figure out a way to convert it to that green paper."

This becomes the key consideration for a deal or no-deal progression.

Project 1

In 2003 my old broker friend John called me and said, "I want you to look at a 40-acre piece of property in Woodland, Cowlitz County." With my aversion to small, in this case very small towns, I did not react. John badgered me once a week for the next two months. Then he called me on a Tuesday and said: "You need to look at this piece by tomorrow. I am signing a listing on Thursday."

I visited the property and John gave me these details: purchase price $2,700.000; down payment at closing $100.000, contract on the balance, full payment due in five years, including simple interest at 4% accruing till contract pay-off.

I said, "Wow!" I asked John to get the listing and I was ready to sign a contract. We recorded it in March 2004. We proceeded with planning the property for residential development.

In mid-2004 I received a call from a broker inquiring if the property was for sale. I said no.

Three months later the same broker called again and insisted on a meeting. He said he would bring his 2 interested buyers. We should state our price. John and I discussed the price we would set; $90,000 per acre or $3.6 million.

We met the offerors and their broker in the broker's conference room. John and I sat on one side of the conference table and the broker and his clients on the other across from us. There was very little polite exchange.

The broker asked the question: "What is your price per acre?"

For a fraction of a minute the past interaction with the broker and his intensifying pressure for a meeting flashed through my mind. Additionally, the offerors seemed to be

nervous. I decided to slow down this nego-
tiation. Easy to do: Increase the asking price
to invite discussion.

I changed my asking price from $90,000
per acre and said: "$102,000 per acre." An
increase of almost one half million dollars.
Out of the corner of my eye I saw John's jaw
drop. I looked across the table. The offerors
said: "Okay."

The balance of the meeting was spent
with defining details.

The contract was executed in November
2004 and fully paid during 2006 to us and
the underlying contract holder.

Conclusion

Sometimes you should follow your hunches and slow things down.

Sometimes you just walk away from negotiations. This event happened in 1987.

I had negotiated with a local property owner, Frank, for almost six months on the purchase of a development site. I finally decided that his price was too high. I told him this story:

A farmer drives his produce to the wholesale market in Chicago very early in the morning. He turns on the radio to listen to the pricing reports. The radio announcer quotes carrots at $0.15 a bundle, onions at $0.09 per pound and lettuce at $0.13 per head.

He arrives at the market and talks to the buyer. The buyer quotes carrots at $0.12 a bundle, onions at $0.07 per pound and lettuce at $0.11 per head.

The farmer replies "but the radio station said it was $0.15 for carrots, $0.09 for onions and $0.13 for lettuce."

The buyer says: "sell them to the radio station."

I said: "Frank, sell your property to the radio station." It is still available.

Rule 7

Define your deal horizon/timing early in the venture

Timing in real estate ventures is as important as location. Repeat: timing in real estate ventures is as important as location.

Zoning codes change. Environmental regulations change. Markets vanish and new ones appear from oversupply to new products. Underwriting parameters for financing change. The cost of funds changes. NIMBY organizations appear and vanish. Litigation takes time and even "successful" lawsuits will impact time.

The impacts on the timeframe of a project can range from simple delay to total demise of a project. Most delays have negative effects on the profitability. If you are lucky, inflation increases profitability.

Project 1

In 1966/67, I was retained to explore the obtaining of a condominium project permit adjacent to one of the Mount Hood ski resorts. The investigation was positive. The zoning code and development codes allowed that type of project.

I recommended to my client to proceed. He hesitated and delayed the decision for two years.

The county elected a new board of commissioners. The overall mood of the board changed to total preservation from the previous philosophy of balanced development. The comprehensive plan and zoning code were revised. The revisions eliminated the possibility of development of a recreational resort.

The project was abandoned.

Project 2

In 2005. two real estate brokers presented me with 27 acres of developable residential land in the City of Battle Ground, Clark County, WA. At about the same time I was approached by a tax consultant to find a land investment for one of his clients. The parcels were impacted by some wetlands. The then governing codes allowed mitigation which appeared to be achievable. Sanitary sewer was represented to be approximately two years in the future.

The client and I formed a partnership. Planning proceeded. In 2007, revisions to the wetland mitigation regulations and classification of wetlands code made it impossible to develop for residential purposes approximately 40% of the parcels' area. In late 2007 it became apparent that a recession was imminent. We delayed further planning and work on the project.

During the recession of 2008/2009, markets crashed for residential development. In 2018 we restarted the project to attempt to recover the partner's capital investment. The results are still out in the future.

Conclusion

Timing is critical in real estate projects. When opportunities for project progress offer themselves take them: secure permits when they are available. The opportunities may not last.

In 1971 we were retained by our client to develop and construct the second mini-storage facility to be built in Oregon.

We had also developed and constructed the first one. At that time zoning codes had not yet made provisions for mini-storages. The product had just been introduced in California. The typical procedure in the county in which the project was to be located required a hearing before the Board of Equalization. We petitioned and scheduled it.

The property on which the storage was to be built straddled two land use zones, "commercial" and "industrial." We needed the use declared appropriate in both in order to build the project. We presented our petition and the argument.

The commissioners discussed the issues from their view for almost one hour. There did not appear to be a clear decision in sight. We had on our team a real estate broker who had just relocated from southern California to Portland, employed by one of the largest brokerages in the USA.

He rose and requested to address the board: "Members of the Board, I represent the largest real property firm in the country. I just relocated from California to Portland. In California, our firm has been involved in the development of 38 mini-storages. They are approximately equally located in industrial and commercial land use zones. Thank you." And he sat down.

It took the board another 10 minutes to approve the use in either or both zones.

After we left the board hearing I asked the broker: "How many of these has your firm done?" He said, "This is the first."

Rule 8

Plan your alternative exit strategies

The logical exit from the project is the sale. Sometimes the sale's results and revenue will be realized in the future. Many contract arrangements that extend into the future sooner or later show some flaws. The original drafters may rely on the mistaken belief that memories of agreements do not fade or get conveniently forgotten. But also, how much time do parties want to spend reviewing every potential event of the future?

During the Japanese asset purchase wave of the 1990s I came across the Japanese practice of performing feasibility analyses projecting 50 years into the future. When I asked the value of it, the answer was "Over a period of 50 years there is at least one recession and one event of war. One should at least formulate contingency plans." Valid reasoning.

Project 1

In 1997, broker John introduced a development project in the city of Ridgefield, Washington. Keep in mind that Ridgefield at that time consisted of a "T" in the road and a tavern, a small cafe, City Hall, and a convenience store. It was showing growth as a bedroom community.

The project needed to be approved as a residential subdivision. I signed a purchase and sale agreement, retained planning and engineering consultants including traffic engineers and environmental scientists.

At the first hearing at the planning commission, I became frustrated with both the presentation of my consultants and their interaction with the planning commission members. The NBA finals were on that night and I decided it was more productive for me to go two blocks to the tavern and watch the game on television than to become totally upset with the procedures at City Hall.

After I reviewed the planning commission discussions and recommendations with my consulting team, I decided that the prospects for success were meager. Within three months I was approached by a CPA/developer who was interested in acquiring a project.

We negotiated a contract acquisition of the project by his entity. We executed a simple one-page letter of understanding which gave me a 25% share of profits upon sale of the project. A very sloppy and poorly defined agreement. It relieved me of any liability and had the prospect of some compensation at some nebulous future time.

The buyer proceeded with the permitting and obtained financing for phase 1 of the 2-phase project. I inquired of the buyer about payment on the memorandum/sharing agreement. He responded: "I don't know when or if I will pay you." I had to act to secure my position in the deal.

The construction loan for the first phase was scheduled to close in one week, on a Wednesday. The tile insurance policy required by the lender was scheduled for issuance for the Monday preceding the closing. On Tuesday I recorded the one-page letter of understanding. The title insurance policy had already been issued. The recording fell into the "title gap." The loan closed, construction and sales went forward. I waited for the next event: 2nd phase financing.

18 months later, I received a call from the CPA: "I need to close the second loan. The bank will not give it to me with your memorandum clouding the title."

I said: "Pay me" and hung up.

We proceeded to mediation. I was paid $250,000 in a settlement. The key to leverage was the title-gap recording of the memorandum. It shifted the control of the deal back to me and gave me a revised successful exit strategy. 23 years later, in 2020, there are still several lots available for houses in the project. The pictured house was just completed.

Conclusion

Explore and execute alternative exit strategies.

The long-term project previously mentioned slopes from the Portland West Hills ridgeline to the west into Washington County. It appeared logical that sanitary sewers should be flowing by gravity to the West and be operated and maintained by the then Washington County Sanitary District. The district resisted to serve the project and refused to accept service to both the project parcels in Washington County and the City of Portland.

I decided to put pressure on the district through an alternative proposal: pumping the sanitary waste east across the West Hills into the Valley adjacent to the Willamette River. I obtained a meeting with Commissioner Mildred Schwab of the City of Portland. I requested a letter from her department that the city would accept our sanitary waste if pumped across the western ridge. She wrote the letter and sent it to me.

My proposal of pumping across an 800-foot high ridge was questionable as to technical and financial feasibility. In other words, it was a bluff.

I submitted the Schwab letter to the Washington County Sanitary District and gave them the choice of the utility revenue from 2,000 residences or loss of it to the City of Portland.

The District saw the light and decided to serve our project.

Rule 9

Be prepared to sell:
any profit is a profit

I sold all my property holdings between 2005 and 2007. I retained one personal residence and the property on which permits were delayed, which made it unsaleable.

The decisions to sell as offers were made on the holdings were not triggered by a vison of things to come in 2007 and forward, but by my conviction that any reasonable profit prospect should always be evaluated. Tax impacts should be factored in but not be the prime trigger in the sell/hold decision.

My decision to sell was strictly fueled by the eagerness of potential buyers to jump into real estate ownership. They were willing to pay prices which resulted in profits for even short-term holdings. There was no crystal ball vision of the pending recession to fuel my decisions to sell. Just pure luck.

Project 1

In 1962 I started to look around for a lot to build a house. I wanted to build in the Portland west hills. I looked for lots which were left unimproved due to difficulties with slope, size, codes, and which might be purchased for an affordable price. I examined and eliminated several prospective sites.

I settled on a lot which was undersized, steeply sloped, triangular, on a steep street.

It also had a magnificent view over down-town Portland, the Willamette River and five Cascade peaks. I developed a site plan and schematic house plan and filed an application for site plan approval with the city. Several neighbors objected with the usual arguments.

The city approved the plans and granted 22 variances to the development code. Over the next 12 months, I constructed a 4-bedroom, 3-bath house.

Total cost: $22,000.

Six months after our move-in my wife called me at my office: "There are three people here, broker and 2 clients, who want to buy our house. Do we want to sell?"

We sold the house to the family for $33,000. A profit of $11,000.

In 1963 this amounted to big money in the single-family market. The same house, prior to its later improvements (which brings its present market value to approximately $1,500,000) would show the equivalent profit of $300,000 on a $900,000 sales price.

Project 2

In 1982 I looked around for another site to repeat my townhouse/condominium project. I found a property in the Portland West Hills which was platted for two separate lots and which might be able to accommodate three residences with the achievable variances and code interpretations. I purchased the property from the owner and proceeded to design.

One mid-morning my secretary came into my office: "There is somebody here to see you." "Who?" "A blue-haired lady in a fur coat who drove up in a blue Cadillac."

I went to meet her in the lobby. Her family's business was a long-term client. "Hello, Mrs. ...... what I can I do for you? Let's sit in the conference room."

After we sat down, she said, "Roland, I do not want you to build on the property diagonally across from my house. I want to buy

it from you. How much do you want for it?"
Just like that.

I thought of what I had in it, $35,000 in acquisition and planning, potential of three units with a profit of $40,000 each, totaling $120,000, consideration of risk, time, her family as a client, etc. I laid that out to her.

All she said: "What's your price?"

I said "$82,000."

She pulled out her checkbook and made out a check for $82,000. "Please get the paperwork done."

Conclusion

Be prepared to act when the opportunity for a deal presents itself.

Two old high school acquaintances meet four years after graduation. Jack is wearing standard work attire for his job at a supermarket. Sam is wearing Gucci loafers, silk shirt and a beautiful suit. Jack asks Sam, "You are doing well. What gives?" Sam:" I am in the used carton business. I buy old boxes for 10 cents each, then sell them at 20 cents each. I make a living on that 10 percent margin."

It is the dollars which count, not the percentages.

Rule 10

Keep it simple

Many real estate deals become more complex as "deal time" lengthens. Buyer requests a modification, seller counters, a few clauses are agreed upon, new conditions may have to be documented, signed around. This all adds complexity, especially when other members of the project team need to be involved. And it adds time to the closing horizon of a transaction. Remember: "time" is also of the essence.

Keep the deal simple.

Project 1

On a weekday in 1977, I received a call from one of my real estate broker acquaintances. "Roland, I need your quick action. I need to close an estate today before 5 p.m. There is an undeveloped commercial property which has not been sold and needs to be."

"I do not have time."

He said, "This piece is worth $80,000. They will take $40,000 cash today."

"What's the address. I will cancel my lunch and go to look at it."

After receiving the address and some size and dimension information, I drove

across town to look at the neighborhood, to-
pography, surrounding streets. I called my
bookkeeper: "How much money do I have in
my account?" There were adequate funds for
the purchase.

I called the broker and told him to pick
up the check at 4 p.m. at my office. I sold the
property the same year for $75,000. A simple
deal.

Project 2

In 1970 an architect who was my client wanted me to look at a gas station which was located adjacent to my and his favorite tavern. It was for sale at what appeared to be a reasonable price.

We made an offer to purchase. Our offer was accepted. We purchased and closed on the site.

We offered the site to the tavern owner, who declined. During the procurement of demolition permits we were approached by an enterprising dentist who wanted to purchase the site and develop his first dental office.

We came to an agreement on sales price and closed the sale for cash. As simple a deal as any.

The office which the Willamette Dental Group developed on the site is still in operation. It is now one of 50 offices the group operates in Oregon, Washington, and Idaho.

And Willamette Dental Group still looks at my teeth at least once a year, although at a different office.

Conclusion

When a deal is simple, move on it.

In 1970 a fellow board member on the Board of Directors of a non-profit organization requested my participation in a brainstorming session with him and his partner.

During one of their winter trips to Palm Desert they came up with the idea to develop a 300-home residential development on 477 acres in the Portland area. I asked them, when they told me of the idea, about the number of afternoon cocktails they had had when that plan became an idea to pursue.

We were engaged to perform a preliminary

feasibility with conceptual numbers and a schematic development plan. The result was a residential development plan ranging from 1,200 to 1,500 residential units depending on the open space and buyer attracting elements and its marketing and sales concept.

The partners retained a San Francisco planning and architectural firm. We were retained as project managers.

When the soils reports indicated potentially unstable soil in the top 12 inches of the site, the San Francisco based architects insisted that 12 inches of topsoil needed to be stripped and removed from 477 acres. Their reasoning: "Garage slabs will be cracking and will need to be replaced." We made the argument that the cost of stripping the soil would far exceed the replacement cost of all garage slabs. Stripping the site did not make sense to us. We lost the argument.

We anticipated this type of conflict to reoccur and resigned as project managers from the project.

Rule 11

Keep control of the deal

In order to keep control of a real estate transaction, you first must come to an agreement which clearly defines price and terms. These include, but are not limited to, price, date of closing, amounts and dates of payments, descriptions of tasks to gauge performance and progress, and their deadlines and procedures for adjustment, i.e. extensions of time.

As many as achievable should be at the sole discretion of the real estate investor.

Control can be easily lost by poorly defined agreement clauses. In most cases, these can be renegotiated and adjusted. At a cost of money and time.

The more serious and fatal events that impact control are decisions by third parties with ultimate decision power, such as regulatory agencies and judicial or quasi-judicial entities. Early negotiations and discussion may avoid some of these impacts. In the case of judicial and quasi-judicial decision-makers, the usual processes of appeal may apply. Sometimes steps outside the procedural thinking may be successful. If you need to terminate a deal, do it fast and early. The first write-off loss is the cheapest.

Project 1

In 1978, after we had sold our office building on Pennoyer Street, we were looking for new quarters for our construction company. We found an "historic house," one of the "historic 19th Street" houses, for lease. We negotiated a multi-year lease and included a purchase option clause for a purchase price of $150,000. We made some tenant improvements and restored the exterior to its original early 20th century appearance. After we moved in, two ladies stopped by to say hello and commend us on the appearance of the building as they remembered it as "little girls." How flattering!

I sold the construction company to three employees in 1979. The building was too large for the new company owners. A broker approached us. He was looking for office space for a law firm. The lawyers had the intent to purchase a building if possible.

I contacted our landlord and gave notice of exercise of our option to purchase. While the option was enforceable, the lease document was not sufficiently concise as to termination and compensation at that event. We renegotiated the purchase option at $250,000 and sold the building to the lawyers for $450,000.

Except for the vague language on lease termination, we had total control of the property through the purchase option.

Project 2

In 1993, an acquaintance who sought my advice from time to time requested my visit to a medium-size Oregon city to review the potential of developing a small downtown parcel.

I could not find a solution for it. I inquired about any other properties. He mentioned a raw land piece of 13 acres located outside the city limits in the surrounding county. After a quick site due diligence analysis, I determined that it needed to be annexed to the city before I would be interested.

In 1997 the request of a client took me again to that city. While there I investigated the status of the 13 acres. It had been annexed to the city.

It also required, for my purposes, a zone change to single-family residential zone and the usual geotechnical investigations, surveys and traffic studies. The process would be handled by a hearings officer.

Upon return to my home office, I called my old acquaintance and asked if the 13 acres were for sale. He said due to a failed earnest money agreement the parcel was now available. At a lunch the next day, I obtained a purchase agreement, payable upon approval of zoning change and traffic impacts.

I obtained OPM from a partner for planning, legal fees, hearings processes, purchase of the property, and buildout of all site improvements for a residential subdivision of small lots. The deal was simple: OPM furnishes all the funds, profits are split 50/50 upon sale of all lots. Except for regulatory approvals, i.e. zone changes and traffic impact reviews, we were in total control.

The hearings proceeded smoothly, there were no major NIMBY objections, the hearings officer notified us of the results: zone change approved, traffic impacts denied, project approval denied.

After my land use attorney called me with that news, I asked to request an extension to review the traffic analysis and re-study the problem for a solution. My attorney called me back: no extension granted. This was on a Tuesday.

On Wednesday I reviewed the developments pending in the same traffic impact area. One was the plan by the school district for an elementary school across the street from our project.

I assumed that its traffic impact issues would be similar to ours.

The only remedy to revise the hearings officer's decision was to file an appeal to the Land Use Board of Appeals, LUBA for short. I called my attorney and confirmed that course of action. Then I instructed her to call the legal counsel of the school district on Thursday to inform the district that we will appeal our decision and also any decision that the school district obtained from its hearings process. Our appeal of the school district's decision would delay the construction of the elementary school at least one year.

My attorney's comment: "You dirty dog!!!."

She called me on Friday afternoon. On other business at the city just before noon she had walked past the open door of a conference room in which the school district's attorney, the hearings officer, the city's risk manager and the city's planning director where huddling. When the school district's attorney saw her walk past the door of the conference room she called her in and asked, "How long an extension do you want to amend the traffic report?" My attorney requested two weeks.

We submitted the revised traffic analysis two weeks forward on Monday morning.

On Tuesday afternoon, the hearings officer issued a 45-page report approving the zone change, the traffic analysis, and all other issues.

There were no other hurdles, the subdivision improvements were constructed and 82 houses were built.

The project was an unqualified success. My partner's and my profits were higher than our pro forma. The elementary school construction proceeded on schedule. The home builder had a built-in market for the families with grade school-age children and sold out the project in 18 months.

The project proceeded only because we kept control through unconventional leverage applied by thinking "outside the box."

Conclusion

Retain control of project process to avoid adversarial decisions and failure.

In 1980 I was induced by an ex-employee to participate in the startup of a new company manufacturing turf and specialty irrigation pump stations. The competitive edge was provided by the component of a "programmable controller" which allowed simulation of startup and operation in the shop rather than the field, cutting installation time from several days to several hours.

Upon my suggestion we also programmed the controller to shut down the pump station operation after six weeks unless a six-digit number eliminated that instruction.

We furnished pump stations to utility districts, golf course contractors and large sports facilities. On two occasions we had not been paid after six weeks. We received irate calls from the contractors that the stations quit running and their grasses were turning brown. It took some explaining that the pump stations required "green paper" to operate. We were paid the next day.

Total control retained.

Restatement: Prerequisites

1. Are you a "Real Estate Deal" personality?
2. Is your "Team" ready?
3. Are your "Partners and Partner Relationships" robust?

Restatement: 11 Simple Rules

1. Do not rely on deals for your living expenses.
2. Do not "need a deal."
3. Use as much OPM as possible.
4. Beware of Small Markets.
5. Be prepared to walk away from a deal.
6. Buy property for less than you think you can sell it.
7. Define your deal horizon/timing early in the venture.
8. Plan your alternative exit strategies.
9. Be prepared to sell: any profit is a profit.
10. Keep it simple.
11. Keep control of the deal.

Epilogue & Summary

The chapters preceding this can be summarized in four comments:

1

"Time" needs to be the essential and total focus in any real estate project, time in all forms: cost of time delays, carrying cost of projects, time of decision to commence, abandon or sell a project. "Time" is truly of the essence.

2

Do not over-emphasize parameters of ROI, IRR in project assessments beyond an initial feasibility analysis. The only criterion which counts in the end: did you make a profit at sale or, if you hold it as investment, is the income exceeding your expenses?

3

Real estate investment requires decisions based on judgment at various phases in the process of going from concept to implementation. The decisions should be more often correct than not. To achieve that result, they need to be based on a record of previous decisions that were born out to have been correct or not.

4

After considering a project and examining its parameters and prospects of success, step back and leave the "box" of thinking in the traditional way of a real estate deal: "Get outside the Box." Here is one amazing example.

Totally Outside the Box

In early 1987, my wife called me in mid-afternoon from her business and said: "Don't be surprised when you come home tonight" and then hung up. Instead of leaving my office at 5:45, I left at 4:45.

This story is about counter-intuitional thinking to do a deal: Thinking counter to the usual logic.

Such a deal most likely contains risk factors, the failure of any would cause the deal to fail.

Deal horizon and sequence of events become critical.

When the opportunity window is short, seize it quickly.

I drove home. We lived in a split–level three-bedroom, two-car garage vanilla house, which we had bought for $85,000 in 1983. Livable, adequate.

Upon arriving the first thing I saw was a

sign at the driveway: "FOR SALE BY OWNER Tel. _____." My wife's car was parked in the driveway.

I walked into the house and asked: "What's the deal?"

"Well, you know that I always wanted to own a house in _____" (she named a planned development on 100 acres around a small lake with 100 houses on half-acre lots). "I found the house I want to buy. It has been vacant and for sale for one year and has not sold. I have gone over there for the past 8 months every day and sat in the back of the house, looking over the lake and at the birds and trees ".

"What is the asking price?" – "$230,000" – I took a deep breath: "That's almost three times the value of this house!" She: "That's right."

"But I am going to buy it for $130,000" she said.

Commentary: In 1987 the real estate housing market was flat, sales were slow. Inflation that would push residential values higher was absent. I/we were in no condition to purchase a more expensive house.

"Where is the money coming from?" I asked.

She: "What is the value of this house?"

I: "$85,000"

She: "What's the mortgage balance?"

I: $50,000"

She: "Do we not own two building lots? What are they worth?"

I: "Together, $45,000"

She: "I am going to sell the house at a discount at $80,000 in two weeks and the lots at $40,000 in two weeks, giving us $70,000 in cash. You just have to get a mortgage for the balance."

I sighed. "Let's go to look at the house."

We could not look at the interior of the house. The neighborhood was beautifully land-scaped. The streets were narrow without curbs, grassy swales separating the lots from the streets. All lots were a minimum size of 20,000 square feet. This house, built in 1973, was a quasi-northwest style/ranch, with low roof lines, large overhangs, two-car garage, tile roof.

The setting was magnificent: the 70-foot long driveway gently sloped down to the house. Two tall Douglas firs were on one side of the driveway, several birch trees on the other. Blooming rhododendrons softened the front elevation of the house behind a barely maintained lawn. The unimproved rear yard sloped approximately 100 feet to the west to the property line, then another 100 feet over common area grass to the edge of the lake. Trees on the far side of the lake obscured the houses located there.

We decided to proceed.

These were the tasks to be successfully completed:

The lots needed to be sold.

Our home needed to be sold.

The offer to purchase the new house needed to be made and accepted.

A mortgage lender needed to be willing to give us a mortgage to cover the cash gap.

My wife made the offer to purchase. $130,000. The broker was reluctant to present such a low offer. The broker's feedback was: "they screamed." They neither rejected nor accepted the offer.

My wife received an offer for $80,000 on our house within 10 days.

I received an offer on the lots for $40,000 in the second week. We accepted the offer on the lots and proceeded to closing.

Two weeks after we had made the offer to

purchase the house, the seller's broker called and indicated that another offer was coming in at $170,000. My wife decided to increase her offer to $173,000. The revised offer was accepted.

It now was up to me to find a lender for a mortgage of $110, 000. One of my lenders from more prosperous times looked at my financial statement, deemed it inadequate for a typical loan commitment, but decided to provide the mortgage loan based on previous performance, not on the strength of my assets.

After closing we moved to the new location.

The immediate changes we made to the house were replacement of the plaid carpet which visually dominated the interior and painting the interior.

After two months, we decided to construct a 2,200 square foot terrace and shading structure to limit the exposure to the westerly sun in the afternoons and evening.

We lived in the house for twelve years. It provided for a pleasant lifestyle and fulfilled my wife's dream-of-a-house. In December 1999, we decided to avoid significant upgrades. We sold in March of 2000.

Financial Results:

Generating the Capital

Sale of house: net proceeds	$30,000
Sale of lots	$40,000
Total Capital	$70,000

Making the Purchase

Source of funds: Total Capital	$70,000
Mortgage Loan	$110,000
Total Purchase, including miscellaneous costs	$180,000
Additional improvements (terrace, rear yard)	$40,000
Total investment in the house	$220,000

(excluding mortgage payments and other
expenditures)

In 2000, after 13 years, we sold the house
for $451,000

Conclusion

The deal had two main components: first,
finding the deal opportunity and, secondly, generating the capital for the deal.

The first component located the object of
purchase, realizing the reason for the absence
of a sale over two years (plaid carpet, dark pan-
eling) and making a quick decision to seize the
opportunity.

The idea for the capital generation in a very
critical, short window by discounting an asset
for cash conversion was the "Out-of-the-Box
Thinking," the essential second component of
this successful deal.

When you identify an opportunity, move on it quickly

Analyze the reasons for the opportunity (perception of correctible defect as a deal killer) and adjust the price of the deal.

Define timelines and act promptly (seller became impatient with the long holding-for-sale period).

Select top location (neighborhood, view).

Do not hesitate to sell when there is an offer for a profit on the table.

In 1987 a Portland attorney called me and requested a conference with his Italian client, about 60 years old, and the client's team. The client had plans to construct a cheese plant in Eugene, Oregon. We had received desired production data and cursory product specifications prior to the meeting. One of my industrial project managers for food processing facilities assembled a project budget: $3,000,000.

The attorney's client immediately focused on the projected cost. "Why does it cost so much?"

"That is what it is going to cost."

More conversations, details, same question. "Why does it cost so much?" This went on a few more times, same question, same answer.

I had to get out of that routine. I had an idea: explain the argument in terms which fit his cultural background and his insights gained in 60 years of life in Italy in the middle of the 20th century.

"Signore, you have led a reasonably long life and acquired much experience, and with it the ability to judge situations quickly?"

"Si, si."

"So have I. Now, when you sit on the Piazza Navona in Rome, sipping an espresso, and you see an elegantly dressed beautiful woman walk by, from your long experience you can judge the investment she requires in attention, maintenance of lifestyle and time in courtship to foster her relationship with you. Yes?"

"Si."

"I have, through years of experience in industrial food processing facilities, acquired the ability to judge a project cost. I can judge the cost of the facility you want to build. Based on my experience my judgment is that its cost is $3,000,000. Can you now agree?"

He emphatically said, *"Si, si, si!"*

That problem was solved. The project never proceeded. Nice to deal with somebody who has experience.

Luck is what happens when
preparation meets opportunities.

Lucius Annaeus Seneca (The Younger)
4 B.C. - 65 A.D.

Roland Haertl's Manifesto

(with inspiration from Ralph Waldo Emerson)

- Be playful and dance through life: laugh and sing with enthusiasm
- Stay young in thought, innovate again and again, yourself and your world.
- Maintain your sense of adventure and curiosity to explore the forever expanding horizons.
- Think outside the box.
- Keep your sense of humor through all adversities.
- Stay optimistic, yesterdays don't define tomorrows.
- Make others happy, it is very rewarding.

- Find and appreciate beauty everywhere, it may require looking longer and harder.
- Opportunities abound in all risks.
- Find the best attributes in others and endeavor to be kind to one another.

Bibliography

I intended to add a lengthy list of books about real estate and how to enter, perform, succeed and fail in the industry. After a short review of my library and a cursory review of the offers in the book markets, I have come to the conclusion that there is only one overriding piece of advice, best expressed by J Scott, eminent house flipper with his wife.

The 100 house rule

He says to look at 100 houses before you make an offer on your first one.

I reviewed and financially analyzed 32 projects before I made the first offer on one. Gaining experience and judgment is more important than all the other elements discussed in the literature.

Contact

This book tells stories about real  estate and formulates some basic axioms and 11 rules that are conclusions based on a lifetime in real estate. Parts of this book are clearly intended to stimulate critical thought about the rules presented and evaluate their validity in everybody's own mind.

In "normal" times I would have presented this book in person at real estate industry meetings and other venues which might be interested in strategies and stories. This is not possible today.

In these unusual times of social distancing during the corona virus pandemic, it occurred to me to provide a channel of communication during self-imposed quarantine and absence of typical socializing.

As an alternative I am offering the email contact below for inquiries, to which I will respond by phone or email. If desired and agreed upon, we can set up a visual conference.

I will be happy to respond to inquiries and engage in discussions of topics.

Roland Haertl
haertlrolandbook@gmail.com